YIELDING TO THE POWER OF GOD

YIELDING
TO THE
POWER OF GOD

Ann Shields

SERVANT BOOKS
Ann Arbor, Michigan

Cover design by Charles Piccirilli

Published by Servant Books
P.O. Box 8617
Ann Arbor, Michigan 48107

Printed in the United States of America
ISBN 0-89283-348-3

87 88 89 90 91 10 9 8 7 6 5 4 3 2 1

YIELDING TO THE POWER OF GOD

One of the most exciting promises in Scripture is, "You will receive *power* when the Holy Spirit comes down on you" (Acts 1:8). Many of us believe this word in faith; this book is for those of us who desire to live out the reality of this word in our relationships, our service, and our personal lives.

What Is Power?

There are different ways to approach the subject of God's power. We could start with the Greek word, *dunamis,* which implies the explosive power of God. It is related unable to exercise these gifts fully.

There are some among you who fear putting yourselves into my hands more than you fear your enemies. I want you to lay aside that fear and timidity. I want you as men and women of courage to deliver yourselves fully and wholeheartedly, eagerly and totally into the hands of your loving God. As you so deliver yourselves into my hands, as you submit yourselves totally to my power, my gifts will flourish among you—my gifts of power and faith and love. My gifts of strength will flourish among you as never before if you have the courage to deliver yourselves fully into my hands.

Are we able to deliver ourselves fully, totally, eagerly, wholeheartedly, into the hands of God? I don't know about you, but I'm not there yet. I want to be, but sometimes I'm afraid of what God might ask. Are you ever afraid of what he might ask of you?

Who is this God who wants us to deliver ourselves fully into his hands? Is he really the God of love, mercy, and justice we declare him to be?

God Knows Us

God knows what each of us needs most. Psalm 139:13 says: "you knit me together in my mother's womb." He knows every part of us. He knew every part of us before we saw the light of day.

I received a great sign that God really knew and loved me when I was baptized in the Holy Spirit. At that time God gave me something I desperately needed. In the three-year period before I was baptized in the Spirit, I had gone through a very difficult time in my life. I had experienced a series of circumstances that involved substantial rejection. I was also disillusioned by my own sinful response to the circumstances. I decided that I wouldn't need anyone or anything; I would handle my life by myself. As a result, I became rather hardened, critical, cynical. I wasn't even certain that God cared. Before long, I lost most, if not all, of my joy and enthusiasm for life. There were times when I could barely make it through the day.

But God continued to draw me to himself even when I wasn't sure whether I believed in him or trusted him. He drew me to himself simply by giving me a desire to surrender my life to him in a way I never had before. Even though I didn't understand what it meant, I prayed such a prayer. And God took me at my word and baptized me in his Holy Spirit. But in addition he gave me what I needed most. He gave me joy which I knew had to be from him. It wasn't dependent upon circumstances, it wasn't dependent upon relationships—none of those had changed. But I knew joy. It was as though someone had taken a pitcher of water and poured it over me. From the tip of my head to the soles of my feet I was flooded with joy. Throughout the sixteen years since —though it has ebbed and flowed at times—I have never lost that joy.

Didn't you experience something like that when you were baptized in his Holy Spirit? Didn't he give you what you needed most at that time?

God Cares About Us

Every time life gets difficult or pressures are great and I begin to wonder, "Where is God in this situation?," I remember he knows me through and through, and I tap back into the first gift—the great joy that he bestowed upon me— and I'm reassured that he loves me personally, intimately, fully.

God knows our deepest needs. He gave us what is ultimately most important: his own Son. All of us have been rescued from the power of sin and death by the death and resurrection of Jesus Christ. In light of this gift, how can we even for a moment doubt the love of God for us?

Is doubt a block that keeps you from experiencing the fullness of his power? In Sirach 2:18 we read that: "equal to his majesty is the mercy that he shows." He who is the mighty God and Prince of Peace, he who is King of Kings and Lord of Lords, is mercy to the same degree. Love and mercy, mercy and love. They are equal to his majesty, his power, his sovereignty, his dominion, his glory. He loves us to the same degree. Don't ever doubt the mercy of God. Don't ever doubt the love of God for you. He's the safest person in the world to trust. How silly we are sometimes to trust others more than we trust God.

God's Justice Draws Us

But while it is true that God is all mercy, he is also a God of justice. Sometimes we have a hard time figuring out how all that goes together, but that's because we are not God. We are human beings. We can't put together mercy and justice. But God joined them together in his son, Jesus Christ.

Sometime ago someone wrote to me and said: "When I hear your strong words, I stop and think: 'They may be strong but they aren't harsh.' No, they're not really harsh. What your strong words are saying is that God loves me so much that he won't tolerate anything in me that keeps me from him."

There may be other, more theological definitions of justice, but I think this is one of the most useful for our purpose here: God loves me so much that he won't tolerate anything in me that keeps me from him.

Sometimes when we experience the discipline of God—when things are hard for us and don't go the way we think they should—we wonder what's happening. But the writer to the Hebrews says that God disciplines us like a father, that he uses all the circumstances in our life to discipline us, to purify us, and to bring us nearer to himself (Heb 12:7-13). None of us can be near him without being made holy as he is holy. His justice expresses his love.

The writer of Hebrews says that all discipline is hard, but later it bears the fruit of justice and peace (Heb 12:11). God's justice is not designed to condemn or destroy us but to bring us to himself.

Several years ago I knew that one of the sins in my life was rash judgment. I didn't judge the people whom I knew well; for them I had a lot of compassion. It was the stranger that I judged. I looked critically at people and speculated about their motives. One day I said to the Lord, "I don't want to be critical anymore because I know that's not the way you are." Then I invited the Lord to do whatever he had to do in order to change me. (If you ever doubt that God answers prayer, try praying that prayer sincerely!)

The next day I was on a plane, and there was a man up the aisle from me with a cup of coffee in his hand, gesturing with his cup. I was sitting behind him, thinking, in my usual fashion, "Look at him. Somebody's going to come down that aisle, he's going to bump them, and somebody's going to get burned.

You'd think he'd be more considerate."

Sure enough. The stewardess came down the aisle, bumped into him, and got burned. I sat there smugly saying, "I knew it, I just knew that was going to happen."

But remember the prayer I prayed? Well, twenty minutes later I got a sudden craving for coffee. I rarely drink it, but God was setting me up. So I asked for a cup of coffee. After I received it from the stewardess, I was holding it in my hand, and a man across the aisle asked me a question. Now, I can't talk without using my hands. So there I was holding the cup of coffee, gesturing with it, when another stewardess came down the aisle, bumped into my cup, and was burned. All I heard from the Lord was, "See?"

I use that example to point out that God loves me so much that he takes me very seriously when I pray to be made more like him. Over the next few years God continued to answer my prayer by allowing me to do *before the day was out* what I had critically judged in another. His discipline was constant until my mind was more conformed to his. When I opened my life to him and said "change me," he took me at my word.

If I am serious about changing, I'll be able to see what he's doing and able to respond to his discipline as a daughter to her father. I don't have to be afraid to deliver myself into his hands because I know that the end result is union with him. The end result is not destruction or condemnation or guilt or separation. The end result is intimate fellowship with the God of heaven and earth.

You've Got to Choose

The second prophecy is rather lengthy and is basically a reprimand to show us how serious God is about this subject.

The prophecy, which was delivered at a meeting of The National Advisory Committee for the Catholic Charismatic Renewal, says:

Hear my word. What I have not accomplished by blessings and gifts, I will accomplish by judgment and purification. My people are in desperate need of this judgment. They have continued in an adulterous relationship with the spirit of the world. They are not only infected with sin, but they teach sin, pamper sin, embrace and dismiss it.

My people who have been blessed by this renewal are more under the spirit of the world than they are under the spirit of my baptism. They are guided by the fear of what others will think of them. They fear failure and rejection in the world, loss of respect by neighbors and superiors and those around them more than they fear me and infidelity to my word.

Therefore your situation is very, very weak. Your power is limited. You are not able to be in the center of the battle. And so a time of judgment and purification must happen. Sin will be called sin. Satan will be unmasked. Fidelity will be held up for what it should be.

There will be purification and persecution among my people. You will have to stand for what you believe. You have to choose between the world and me. You have to choose whose words you will follow and whom you will respect. And in that choice what has not been accomplished by the blessings and gifts I have given will be accomplished by discipline. What has not been accomplished in the baptism and the flooding of the gifts of my Spirit will be accomplished in the baptism of fire. The fire will move among you and burn away what is chaff. The fire will move among you individually, corporately, and around the world. I will not tolerate the situation as it now is. I will not tolerate the adulterous mixing of my gifts and blessings with infidelity and sin.

What you need to do is come before me in total submission to my word. What you need to do is drop those things that are your own—those things of the past. What you need to do is see yourselves and those for whom you have responsibility in light of this hour of judgment and purification. You need to do for them what will best help them to stand strong and be faithful servants. There will be casualties. It will not be easy, but it is necessary. It is necessary that my people be, in fact, my people. That my church be, in fact, my church. That my spirit, in fact, bring forth purity of life, purity and fidelity to the gospel.

There's a great deal that could be said about that prophetic word. But I want to underscore just a few of the most important points.

No More Fence Straddling

The Father said to us in that prophecy that we have to choose between the world and him. I believe that we have done too much fence straddling. On one hand, we want some things from the world; on the other, we want the gifts and life and power of the Holy Spirit. We want what we think is the best of both worlds. We tolerate things God doesn't want us to tolerate.

But to choose the Father and his baptism is to make a real break with sin and the sinful ways of the world. Because of the baptism in the Holy Spirit and because of the gifts that he has poured out upon us, our lives should look very different. We should put aside ambition and pride and jealousy. Sometimes those are the very sins that we carry right into the prayer meeting, the renewal center, the service team. We cannot take the gifts he's given us and use them for our own advancement.

We are servants of the master, and the gifts he's given must be used only for his purposes. If God chooses to raise us up, blessed be God. But that cannot be our goal or our desire, and we need to examine our motives very carefully. We need to examine the motives for our leadership, the motives for exercising gifts. Do I do this for the glory of God, or do I do it for my own?

We are warned so clearly in Scripture that on the last day there will be those who stand before him saying, "Lord, Lord, have we not prophesied in your name? Have we not exorcised demons by its power? Did we not do many miracles in your name as well?" And he will reply, "I never knew you. Out of my sight, you evildoers!" (cf., Mt 7:22, 23). We need to come humbly before God, asking him to teach us. We should hold the gifts he's given us very, very lightly in our hands, realizing that he is the owner, not us. He is the one who says how, when, and where they get used.

It's a hard word. But it comes from a Father who has given us the best of what he has and who knows the richness of life we will receive if we use those gifts according to his purpose.

Distracted by the Pleasures of This World

One way to examine our lives in light of this prophecy is to take a look at Luke 8:11-15. It's the very familiar parable of the seed and the sower:

This is the meaning of the parable. The seed is the word of God. Those on the footpath are people who hear, but the devil comes and takes the word out of their hearts lest they believe and be saved. Those on the rocky ground are the ones who, when they hear the word, receive it with joy. They have no root; they believe for a while, but fall away in time of temptation. The seed fallen among briers are those who hear, but their progress is stifled by the cares and riches and pleasures of life and they do not mature. The seed on good ground are those who hear the word in a spirit of openness, retain it, and bear fruit through perseverance.

The cares and riches and pleasures of life—think about this for a moment.

It's true that God created this world. It's true that all that God created was good. And God created much for us to enjoy. But because of the fall and because of Satan who prowls around trying to destroy us, some of the things of this world are infected by sin so that they draw us away from God. We've got to look at our relationships, our forms of entertainment, the use of our money and say, "Does this draw me away from God or bring me closer to him?"

This prophetic word is a word of purification. What is it in our lives that chokes out the word of God? What doesn't allow the word of God to take root? What keeps us from responding consistently to the word of God? What is it? We need to decide to root it out. Not tomorrow or the next day or next week or next year, but *now*. What God has for us is so much better than the pleasures we cling to in order to get through the pressures and tensions of life.

Of course, there are some pleasures and joys that God certainly
intends us to have. He wants us to
enjoy the beauty of his creation. He
wants us to enjoy the brothers and
sisters he's given to us. He wants us
to be able to enjoy the talent that
flows from the hands of our brothers and sisters in art, music, litera-
ture, and so much more. God
intends us to enjoy them. But there
are forms of all those things that
are infected by sin and which therefore draw us away from God. Let's
turn away from them.

That's what God is saying in this
word. He won't tolerate the mixture
anymore. We've got to choose.

Distracted by the Cares
of This Life

I also believe God wants to purify
us from anxiety about the cares of
this life.

Many of us are burdened with

anxieties and difficulties. We all have cares and worries and concerns. But do we act as though we don't have God? Do we act as though the responsibility for all those burdens and cares is ours and that we have to work out solutions alone? Or do we believe that we have a God who will meet our needs? He has promised to supply what we need in Jesus Christ. Do we believe that? Or do we act like unbelievers? Are we torn by anxiety and fear and worry about our children, our marriage, other circumstances in our families, our business? Do we wonder: "How much longer am I going to have a job?" or think "I don't have a job, what am I going to do? How am I going to meet the bills? How am I going to care for my children? How am I going to handle a child who is chronically ill? How am I going to meet those needs? What am I going to do?"

We have legitimate needs, yet we

so easily act like unbelievers who have no loving Father. We need to live like people who are confident that we have a Father in heaven, one who clothes and cares for the birds of the air and the lilies of the field—and one who most certainly will care for us. "O weak in faith!" Jesus chided (Mt 6:30).

We are not characters on the afternoon soap operas whose lives go from bad to worse and who have to manage everything on their own. That's not what God intended for his children. He wants us to come to him with our burdens and our anxieties, with our cares and our concerns. He wants us to lay them at his feet.

One woman told me about a period in her life where she had gone through enormous financial stress. One day, in prayer, she was thanking the Lord for providing what money she needed for that week. Then she said, "Lord, if only I could have a few flowers, they would lift my spirit! I don't know how to ask you because you've already done so much but, oh, it would help me so." That evening outside her apartment door was a window box of flowers from a neighbor with a note that simply said, "God told me to give you this." God knows. God cares if only we turn *to him* with our needs.

A man told me a somewhat similar story of not having money to pay a bill that had to be sent. He found in his mailbox an envelope containing no note but the exact amount of money needed. God does expect us to be responsible, carrying out to the best of our ability the obligations we have assumed. But when we've done that and are still in need, he wants us to turn to him asking for help.

God says in this prophecy that we who have been especially blessed through renewal are still influenced more by the spirit of the world—in this case by fear, anxiety, and timidity—than by the Spirit of his baptism. We need to change that. We need to move more and more into trusting our heavenly Father.

Be Zealous for Purity

In the prophecy the Lord says that his purifying fire will move among us. For those who are repentant, I think it will be the fire of his love. But for those who are not repentant, I believe it will be the purging fire of God's judgment. I want to repent as often as I need to. I want to experience that warming fire of his love, and I want to bring as many other people to repentance as possible so that they can experience the fire of his love. Don't you?

Don't be afraid to face your own sin. Admit it, repent for it. Go to confession and receive grace and power to change. Don't be afraid to speak truth to those in your prayer groups and families and, *where you are responsible,* churches. What is worse: to have them angry with you, or to have God angry at them?

John Wesley said, "Give me a hundred men [and I'll add women] who fear nothing but God, who hate nothing but sin, and who know nothing but Jesus Christ and him crucified, and I will shake the world." Who wants to shake the world, brothers and sisters? Ask yourself: do you fear nothing but God, hate nothing but sin, and know nothing but Jesus Christ and him crucified? God wants a pure people. God wants a people who really are willing to make war against sin in all the ways that it manifests itself in their lives. Check yourself. Where are you?

Holiness and Power Are Inseparable

Finally, I want to quote a portion of another prophecy that was deliv-

ered at a later National Advisory
Committee meeting:

My holy work requires a holy
people. Heed this word. Holy,
holy, holy is the Lord. Holy, holy,
holy are his ways. Holy, holy, holy
are his works. Holy, holy, holy
must his people be. No longer will
I tolerate compromise.

Be holy in your very breathing,
for I have breathed upon you my
most Holy Spirit. This breath is
the breath of fire that purges
unto holiness. This breath is the
breath of life that makes things
new. Do not smother this breath
of purification, this breath of my
Holy Spirit.

Reverence your baptism in my
Holy Spirit. Be true, be true, be
true to the gift of my own holiness. My power is held back
because my holiness and my
power are one. You have blocked
my holiness in your lives and so
you have blocked my power. Why

do you weary me with your pleas for more power when you have my answer before you? Be holy as your Father in heaven is holy.

Holiness and power are inseparable. In some ways we've settled for a compromise in our lives. We allow things in our lives that *we* don't think are that big or noticeable, and yet God says, "No compromising."

Single-Mindedness

God wants us to be single-minded and single-hearted for him and his ways. That is another way of saying he wants us to stop straddling the fence. He wants both feet in his camp.

A year ago I was riding home from mass with a family. It was December 8, and the homily had called us to be single-minded for God as Mary is single-minded for God.

While we were riding along, the

seven-year-old son said, "Dad, what does 'single-minded' mean?" His father was trying to explain, when the older brother spoke up. He was only nine, but he said, "You know what I think it means? It means that your mind isn't like a pigpen."

None of us adults could have said it better. It's worth asking ourselves whether our mind is like a pigpen. Are we so cluttered up with junk and compromise that it's hard for us to hear God? When we can't hear God speak, it's very hard for us to act cleanly and purely in the power of God.

Paul says in 2 Corinthians 10:5 that we are to "bring every thought into captivity to make it obedient to Christ." That's a pretty high call, but it is possible because of grace. God's word is true, so if Scripture calls us to it, then it is possible. But it takes purification and self-discipline; it takes really putting our minds under the Lordship of Jesus Christ.

But that's what we want to be: single-minded and single-hearted for the ways of God. Only then can God's power really work through us. Only then will we act more like God and think more like God, the prerequisites for experiencing his power.

In my own life, God has had to do a lot of purification, discipline, and training to get me to be obedient to him. I want my strongest desires to be to love God and to make him known. That's what I really want.

The Grace to Be Made More Holy

God never asks us to do something that he has not already given us the ability to do. The *Living Bible* translates 2 Corinthians 8:12 this way: "God wants you to give what you have, not what you haven't." Paul was encouraging the Corinthian believers to be generous in their financial sharing with the needy Christians in Jerusalem. But the principle holds true for anything God asks from us. He will provide the grace we need to trust him and deliver ourselves into his hands. There is great grace available to us to help us face our sin and to make a firm and clear decision against compromise with sin.

Sometimes we fear surrendering ourselves to God because we think God is going to ask something of us that we can't or don't want to give him. I remember one particular dramatic lesson God taught me about this.

I had been part of the community in Steubenville from its beginning in 1977. I loved being there; I loved being a part of that people. I was sure God intended me to work in the University of Steubenville for the rest of my life. It was all I wanted.

Then one day I was asked if I would consider moving to Ann Arbor, Michigan, for a couple of years. My immediate reaction was negative. Why should I move? I was comfortable where I was. God was blessing my ministry. I didn't want to have to get to know new people. Out of my fear, I said, "The idea couldn't be from God. If God were asking this of me, I'd have a lot more peace and joy about it."

I tried to set the question aside with that bit of rationalization, but somewhere deep within my spirit God let me know that moving to Ann Arbor *was* part of his will for me. It was a matter of my trust in his care. Finally, I went back to those who had offered this opportunity to me and said, "Yes, it's God's will. I'll go."

But then a friend of mine said, "Isn't it hard for you to make this kind of a change?" And I said, "Yes, it's very hard. I really don't want to do it, but it's the will of God." I must have sounded like a martyr at the time, but I thought I was being very, very generous.

Another good friend was listening

and said, "I've often heard you teach how God's will is a manifestation of his love. If that's so—and I believe it is—then how can his will not be *your preference?*"

I knew she was right, and the truth really penetrated my heart. But I didn't like it, so I said, "What are you trying to do, squeeze blood out of a stone? I've already said 'Yes.' How can I like something I don't like?"

"But if you believe God's will is the most loving thing for your life, and you still prefer something else, that just doesn't make sense."

I knew this was true. But the logic of it was little comfort. God was going to have to work some greater grace in me before I could "like something I didn't like." So, I went before him and said, "Lord, I still have my preferences, but I really do believe that you love me. I really do believe that your will is the most loving thing for my life, so I'm going to close the door on my preferences." In other words, I chose not to think about them anymore.

Parenthetically, I want to say that preferences can have an important place in discerning God's will. God can speak through them at times. But, once we *know* his will, then it's time to close the door on our preferences that don't fit with his will.

So I said, "Lord, I'm going to do what you want, and I'm going to shut the door on my preferences." God was more present to me then than I had ever experienced before. I knew he was right there. I could almost see him. In my heart, I heard him say, "I love you so much that if I could bring you home with me right now, I would. But the Father has much work for you to do." And in that moment, I knew intimacy. I knew the desire of the Son to have me with him. He, the Lord of heaven and earth, wanted to be with me. I can't begin to convey to you what that kind of intimacy with God did for me. I wanted to say, "Ask more of me. Let me give up more of my preferences that I might have more of you." And over the years, God has done exactly that. God cannot be outdone in generosity.

Are you afraid of something that God might ask of you? If you experience fear and doubt, just place yourself before God and ask for the grace. God will give it. The Lord has said in Luke 6:38, "Give, and it shall be given you. Good measure pressed down, shaken together, running over, will they pour into the fold of your garment. For the measure you measure with will be measured back to you." If we give all, God gives all. If we give him the right to purify us, the freedom to root out our sin and change us completely, then he will give himself unreservedly to us. And then we know true power.

A Response of Surrender

I encourage you to pray a prayer of surrender like the following one:

Lord Jesus, you have been incredibly generous with me. In dying for me, you have secured forgiveness for my sins and have opened the gates of heaven to me. You have poured out upon me new life in your Holy Spirit. You have showered me with gifts and graces and many other blessings.

I want to respond generously, too. I want to surrender my life to you. I want the light of your truth to penetrate any darkness in my life. I'm ready to face my sin and see my motives. If there is anything that keeps me apart from you or hinders me from fully living your life, I want it purified.

I want you to enter in and take possession of this life that is already yours. I want you to rule and reign over me completely. I want to be holy so that your power might flow through me, so that men and women everywhere might come to know how much you love them and that they too might give their lives to you.

Hear my prayer, and let my cry come unto you. Amen.

That, brothers and sisters, is the way to yield to and to know the power of God.